BATS
Nature's
FRIENDS
by Joyce Markovics
NORWOOD HOUSE PRESS
T0378448

Norwood House Press

For more information about Norwood House Press, please visit our website at:
www.norwoodhousepress.com or call 866-565-2900.

Book Designer: Ed Morgan
Editorial and Production: Bowerbird Books

Photo Credits: Rene Riegal/Unsplash.com, cover; Thomas Lipke/Unsplash.com, cover; Joe McGowan/flickr, 4; Bureau of Land Management/flickr, 5; freepik.com, 6 left; Joe McGowan/flickr, 6 right; © MerlinTuttle.org, 7; freepik.com, 8; Wikimedia Commons, 9; © MerlinTuttle.org, 10; flickr, 11; Bureau of Land Management/flickr, 12; Bureau of Land Management/flickr, 13; freepik.com, 14; Wikimedia Commons, 15 bottom left; Wikimedia Commons, 15 bottom right; © MerlinTuttle.org, 16; © MerlinTuttle.org, 17; © MerlinTuttle.org, 18; © iStock.com/AWelshLad, 19; © iStock.com/sasimoto, 19; © MerlinTuttle.org, 21; Boudewijn Huysmans/Unsplash.com, 22; Bernard DUPONT/flickr, 23; USFWS/flickr, 24; © MerlinTuttle.org, 25; USFWS/flickr, 26–27; freepik.com, 29.

Hardcover ISBN: 978-1-68450-767-2
Paperback ISBN: 978-1-68404-776-5

Library of Congress Cataloging-in-Publication Data

Names: Markovics, Joyce L., author.
Title: Bats / by Joyce Markovics.
Description: Chicago : Norwood House Press, [2023] | Series: Nature's friends | Includes bibliographical references and index. | Audience: Grades 2-3
Identifiers: LCCN 2021057773 (print) | LCCN 2021057774 (ebook) | ISBN 9781684507672 (hardcover) | ISBN 9781684047765 (paperback) | ISBN 9781684047826 (ebook)
Subjects: LCSH: Bats--Juvenile literature.
Classification: LCC QL737.C5 M3624 2023 (print) | LCC QL737.C5 (ebook) | DDC 599.4--dc23/eng/20211217
LC record available at https://lccn.loc.gov/2021057773
LC ebook record available at https://lccn.loc.gov/2021057774

353N—082022

Manufactured in the United States of America in North Mankato, Minnesota.

CONTENTS

Millions of Bats 4

Bat Facts 8

Echo Makers 12

Skeeter Eaters 14

Plant Farmers 16

Bat Poop 20

At Risk 22

A World without Bats 26

Nurture Nature: Build a Bat Habitat! 28

Glossary 30

For More Information 31

Index 32

About the Author 32

MILLIONS OF BATS

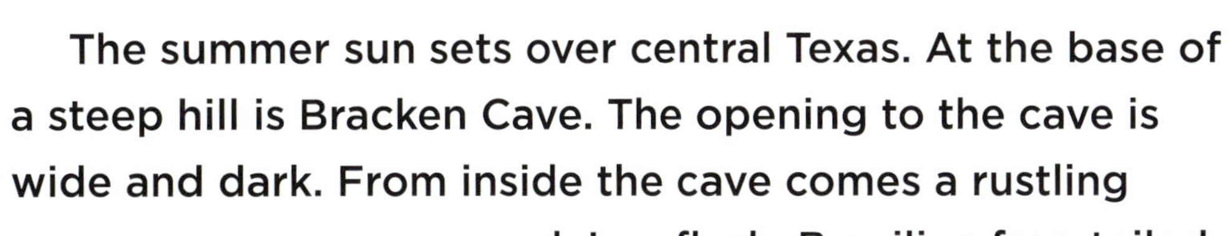

The summer sun sets over central Texas. At the base of a steep hill is Bracken Cave. The opening to the cave is wide and dark. From inside the cave comes a rustling sound. In a flash, Brazilian free-tailed bats start whizzing out of the cave. More and more appear. Soon, millions of bats are spiraling into the sky like a bat tornado.

A Brazilian free-tailed bat

For almost four hours, the bats fly out of the cave. In all, there are almost twenty million of them! “Bracken Cave is the largest **colony** of bats in the world,” says Fran Hutchins. Fran works at Bracken Cave.

Bracken Cave is near the city of San Antonio, Texas.

Brazilian free-tailed bats live in North, Central, and South America.

Where are the bats going? They fly to nearby farmland to look for **insects**. Brazilian free-tailed bats are fast flyers. They swoop and dive to catch flies and moths. In one night, a bat can eat its body weight in bugs. The entire bat colony **devours** "100 tons of bugs every night," says Fran. That's more than the weight of a space shuttle!

Brazilian free-tailed bats can fly up to 100 miles per hour (160 kph)!

Most of the bats are new moms. Back at the cave are millions of hungry mouths for them to feed. The ceiling of the cave is a big bat **nursery**. It's covered with pink, hairless baby bats. After feeding all night, the mother bats return to their babies. They feed the baby bats, called pups, milk from their bodies.

Dozens of baby pink bats hang from the ceiling of Bracken Cave. Mother bats can identify their babies by scent.

BAT FACTS

Bats are **mammals** like dogs and humans. However, they're the only mammals that can truly fly. There are about 1,400 different kinds of bats. Most are nocturnal, or active at night. The biggest are fruit bats. They look a lot like foxes with large wings. They have big eyes and superb eyesight. Fruit bats live in **tropical** places. Their favorite foods are fruit and **nectar** from flowers.

The largest fruit bat has a wingspan of 6 feet (1.8 m).

Vampire bats usually feed on livestock, such as cows and pigs, or birds—not people.

A few bats eat fish or frogs. Fishing bats fly over water and grab fish with the claws on their feet. One well-known group of bats feeds on blood! However, vampire bats don't suck blood. They bite an animal's skin with their razor-sharp teeth. Then they lick up the blood with their tongues.

Bats have lived on Earth for more than fifty million years!

About seventy percent of all bats eat insects. In the United States, of the forty-seven bat **species**, forty-two are bug eaters. They feed on all kinds of insects, from beetles to mosquitoes. Bats have wings that are like giant hands. Stretched across their wings is thin, strong skin. The wing skin connects to the back and rear legs. Bats use their wings not only to fly but also to scoop up bugs in flight.

A bat carries a scorpion it has just caught.

During the summer and fall, **insectivorous** bats eat as much as they can. They're building up fat. Why? Many species **hibernate** in winter. They need the extra fat to survive months of cold weather in some parts of the world. Other bats migrate. They travel to warmer places to find food.

This bat is hibernating.

A bat's wings are covered in tiny bumps called Merkel cells. Each bump has hair growing out of it. The hairs help the bat sense the flow of air. This helps the bat fly faster and more easily!

ECHO MAKERS

A bat zeros in on its insect dinner

Insect-eating bats have an amazing skill. It's called echolocation (ek-oh-loh-KAY-shuhn). Using their mouths, these bats make high-pitched sounds. The sounds bounce off things. Then they return to the bats as **echoes**. This allows bats to "see" in the dark without using their eyes. Once a bat locates an insect, it chomps down on it in midair!

Bats have amazing hearing too.

However, a bat with a full mouth can't echolocate. So some bats make sounds with their noses! They may have sword-shaped or frilly noses. These strange nose shapes help the bats echolocate when they're eating.

Insect-eating bats are not blind. They see in black and white.

SKEETER EATERS

Echolocation allows bats to catch tons of insects. Many of these insects are bloodsucking mosquitoes. A colony like the one in Bracken Cave in Texas can eat 500,000 pounds (226,796 kg) of mosquitoes per night. Mosquitoes are the most dangerous creatures on Earth. They spread deadly diseases, like malaria and yellow fever. These bugs kill two to three million people each year. In fact, mosquitoes have killed as many as fifty billion people throughout history. By eating harmful mosquitoes, bats help people.

A cloud of bats flying over farmland

Bats can also help control other insect pests. Many farmers use **pesticides** to protect their crops from hungry insects. Bats, however, are a natural pesticide. They eat bugs, such as moths, that attack corn and cotton plants. A single female moth can lay 1,000 eggs. For example, if a bat eats one moth, a pecan farmer might get 100 more pecans. Over time, that adds up to a lot of pecans.

A mosquito drinking a person's blood

Some baby moths, like this one, eat crops.

PLANT FARMERS

Fruit-eating bats are hugely important too. They use their noses and sharp eyesight to find ripe fruit. Once they do, they slurp up the fruit. Then the bats spit out the **pulp** and seeds. Fruit bats fly from tree to tree. Along the way, they spread the seeds. This helps new plants grow. Some bats swallow fruit seeds. Amazingly, a few kinds of seeds will only grow after they've passed through a bat's body!

A fruit-eating bat flies off with a ripe fig

Other bats drink sweet flower nectar. These bats often have long noses and thin tongues. They will hover near a flower like a little helicopter. With their tongues, they lap up the nectar. As they feed, they're doing the plants a big favor.

This bat is about to drink nectar from a bloom.

While they're feasting, yellow pollen from the flowers sticks to the bats' fuzzy fur. Pollen helps plants **reproduce**. Bats carry pollen from bloom to bloom. As they do, the powdery pollen rubs off on flowers. This allows the plant to make seeds that, over time, become new plants.

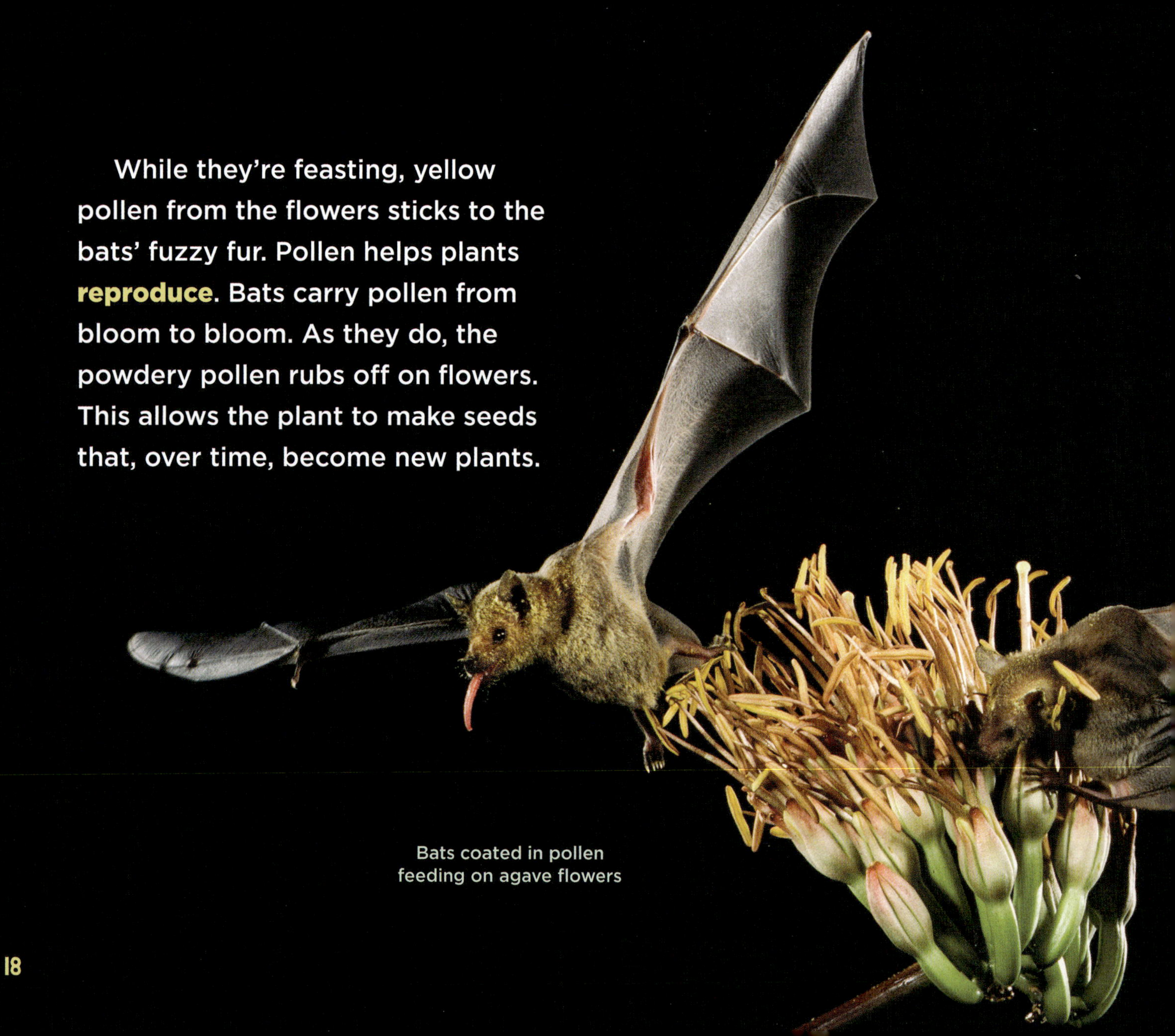

Bats coated in pollen feeding on agave flowers

Bats **pollinate** flowering plants and fruit trees. In all, more than 500 kinds of plants depend on bats for pollination. These include balsa, banana, and date trees as well as agave plants.

A bat named the lesser long-nosed bat has its own favorite food—cactus flowers. Some cactus flowers bloom for just one night in spring. The long-nosed bat knows exactly when this happens. After it finds a flower, it drinks its nectar. By the following day, the blossom has closed!

A cactus flower

BAT POOP

Bats also make something that people can use—guano (GWAH-noh)! Guano is bat poop. It's one of the world's best fertilizers. When added to soil, it makes the soil richer. Farmers use fertilizer to help their crops grow bigger and healthier. People have known the value of guano for hundreds of years. The ancient **Inca** valued guano so much that they forbid their people from harming bats.

Lots of bat guano

Bat guano consists of fine bits of insects and natural chemicals. It's also packed with **microbes**. These tiny living things can help break down just about anything. They can even tackle **toxic** materials. The microbes in bat guano have also been used to develop **antibiotics** for people!

A bat approaches a pitcher plant. The inside of the pitcher is a fluid-filled cup. The bat sleeps inside the cup above the fluid.

Bats in Borneo use the pitcher plant as a toilet. In exchange for a safe place to sleep, the bats poop inside the plant, giving it nutrients.

AT RISK

Despite all they do, bats face serious risks. Every day, their **habitats** are being destroyed. People chop down the forests where bats live to build farms and new towns. People also disturb caves and other places where bats **roost** or hibernate. When a bat is awakened in this way, it uses up a lot of energy. This can result in the bat's death.

Humans destroy forests by cutting down trees.

Another problem affecting bats is fear. People wrongly think that many bats carry diseases. The truth is only a tiny percentage of bats can make people sick. Also, some people think that all bats are vampire bats. They mistakenly believe that vampire bats feed on humans. Because of this, people often kill entire colonies of bats.

A colony of Seba's short-tailed bats roosts in a building.

In some parts of the world, fruit bats are hunted for food. Hunting further reduces the bat population.

In North America, something else is killing bats. It's called white-nose syndrome (WNS). This deadly disease is caused by a kind of **fungus**. Bats that have WNS get white, fuzzy growths on their noses, ears, and wings. The disease triggers the bats to wake up from hibernation. Then they use up their stored energy and can starve to death.

This little brown bat has white-nose syndrome.

WNS was first discovered in a cave in New York in 2006. In recent years, it's been found throughout the United States and Canada. Bats often catch WNS from other bats. Some bats suffer more than others. Little brown and Indiana bats, for example, are likely to be harmed by the disease. To date, WNS has killed millions of cave-dwelling bats.

This is a colony of highly endangered Indiana bats.

People can spread the disease to bats too. They can track WNS fungus on their shoes or clothing when they enter a cave.

A WORLD WITHOUT BATS

What if there were no bats? Many things would happen. There would be many more insect pests, like mosquitoes. There might also be more crop-eating bugs. In addition, many of the fruits that bats pollinate would be hard to find. On top of that, the plants that depend on bats to spread their seeds could die off. Also, no more bat guano means less fertilizer for farmers.

Bats leaving Bracken Cave

Fran Hutchins still gets goosebumps watching the millions of bats at Bracken Cave. "It's one of those jobs where you just can't believe you get to do this for work."

What can people do to help bats? Bats need more places to live. So, people can install bat houses in their yards or neighborhoods. Or they can join a bat club, like Merlin Tuttle's Bat Conservation or Bat Conservation International. Both groups work to protect bats and their habitats. Spread the word about how incredible bats are!

BUILD A BAT HABITAT!

Different bat species live in different habitats, including forests, deserts, and caves. Pick a bat and learn about its home. Then build a diorama showing the bat in its habitat.

- Choose one kind of bat and research where it lives.
- Next, gather supplies to build a diorama of its habitat. Look for a cardboard box, markers, colored paper, scissors, tape, and fishing line or yarn.
- Make the inside of the box look like the bat's habitat.
- Finally, create a small model of the bat species you chose and include it in your diorama.

PRESENT YOUR DIORAMA TO A FRIEND OR ADULT. TELL THEM ALL ABOUT THE AMAZING BAT YOU CHOSE AND ITS HABITAT!

GLOSSARY

antibiotics (an-ti-bye-OT-iks): medicines used to stop the growth of disease-causing bacteria.

colony (KOL-uh-nee): a large group of animals that live together.

devours (di-VOURZ): eats hungrily and quickly.

echoes (EK-ohz): sounds that bounce off an object and return to the place where they came from.

fungus (FUHN-guhss): a plantlike organism that can't make its own food.

habitats (HAB-uh-tats): places in nature where animals normally live.

hibernate (HYE-bur-nate): to go into a sleeplike state during periods of cold weather.

Inca (ING-kuh): belonging to South American Indian peoples.

insectivorous (in-sek-TIV-er-uhs): specialized to feed on insects.

insects (IN-sekts): small animals that have six legs, three body parts, two antennas, and a hard covering.

mammals (MAM-uhlz): warm-blooded animals that have hair or fur and nurse their babies.

microbes (MYE-krohbz): extremely tiny living things that can only be seen with a microscope.

nectar (NEK-tur): a sweet liquid made by plants.

nursery (NUR-suh-ree): a place for young animals.

nutrients (NOO-tree-uhnts): substances needed by plants to grow and stay healthy.

pesticides (PESS-tuh-sidz): chemicals that kill insects and other pests that damage crops.

pollinate (POL-uh-nayt): to carry pollen from one flower to another, which fertilizes the second flower, allowing it to make seeds.

population (pop-yuh-LAY-shuhn): the number of people or animals living in a place.

pulp (PUHLP): the soft, wet part of fruit.

reproduce (ree-pruh-DOOS): to have offspring.

roost (ROOST): to rest or sleep in a particular place.

species (SPEE-sheez): types of animals or plants.

toxic (TOK-sik): poisonous or deadly.

tropical (TROP-i-kuhl): having to do with the warm areas of Earth near the equator.

FOR MORE INFORMATION

Books

Carney, Elizabeth. *Bats*. Washington, DC: National Geographic, 2010.
Readers will learn fascinating bat facts.

Somervill, Barbara A. *Vampire Bats: Hunting for Blood*. New York, NY: Rosen Publishing, 2012.
This book explores the life cycles and habitats of vampire bats.

Taylor, Marianne. *Bats: An Illustrated Guide to All Species*. Washington, DC: Smithsonian Books, 2019.
Read this book to learn all about different bats.

Websites

Bat Conservation International: Bat Squad
(https://www.batcon.org/about-bats/games-and-activities/bat-squad/)
Find out how to help bats.

Merlin Tuttle's Bat Conservation
(https://www.merlintuttle.org)
Learn about bats and bat conservation.

Woodland Park Zoo: Bat Conservation
(https://www.zoo.org/batconservation)
Readers can learn about threats to bats and how to help save these animals.

INDEX

bats,
  Brazilian free-tailed, 5, 6
  colonies, 5, 6, 14, 23
  diet, 8, 9, 10, 11, 16, 17, 19
  eyesight, 8, 12, 13, 16
  fishing, 9
  flying foxes, 8
  fruit, 8, 16, 17, 19, 23, 26
  guano, 20, 21, 26
  habitats, 22, 27
  hunting, 23
  noses, 13, 16, 19, 24
  pups, 7
  roosts, 22
  teeth, 9
  vampire, 9, 23
  wings, 8, 10, 11, 24
Bracken Cave, 5, 14, 26
echolocation, 12, 13, 14
farmers, 15, 20, 26
hibernation, 11, 22, 24
Hutchins, Fran, 5, 6, 26
insects, 6, 10, 11, 12, 13, 14, 15, 21, 26
mammals, 8
Merlin Tuttle's Bat Conservation, 27
migration, 11
mosquitoes, 10, 14, 26
nectar, 8, 17, 19
pesticides, 15
pollination, 18, 19, 26
seeds, 16, 18, 26
Texas, 5, 14
white-nose syndrome (WNS), 24, 25

ABOUT THE AUTHOR

Joyce Markovics has written hundreds of books for kids. She loves wildlife and is especially batty about bats. Joyce lives in an old, creaky house along the Hudson River. She hopes the readers of this book will take action—in small and big ways—to protect nature, one of our greatest gifts. Joyce lovingly dedicates this book to a friend and new mother bat, Heather, and her bat pup, Hazel.